THE PAJAMA GAME

Words and Music by

Richard Adler & Jerry Ross

ISBN 978-1-4950-9368-5

7777 W. BLUEMOUND RD. P.O. BOX 13819 MILWAUKEE, WI 53213

In Australia Contact:
Hal Leonard Australia Pty. Ltd.
4 Lentara Court
Cheltenham, Victoria, 3192 Australia
Email: ausadmin@halleonard.com.au

Visit Hal Leonard Online at
www.halleonard.com

HEY THERE

Words and Music by RICHARD ADLER
and JERRY ROSS

HERNANDO'S HIDEAWAY

Words and Music by RICHARD ADLER
and JERRY ROSS

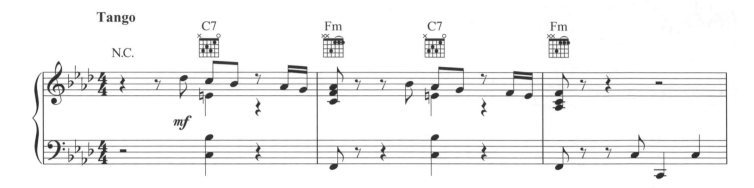

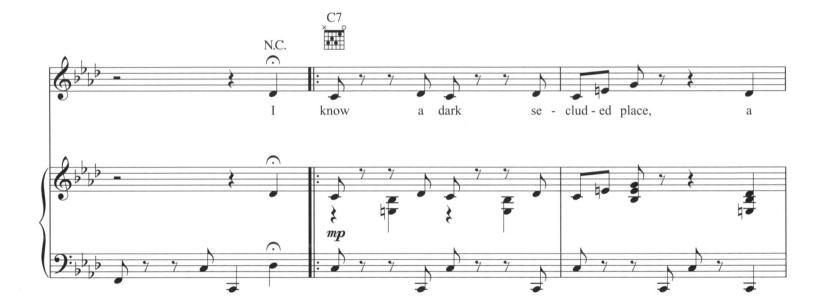

I know a dark se - clud - ed place, a

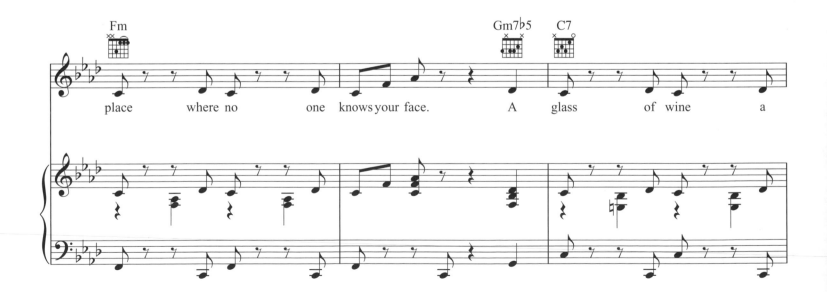

place where no one knows your face. A glass of wine a

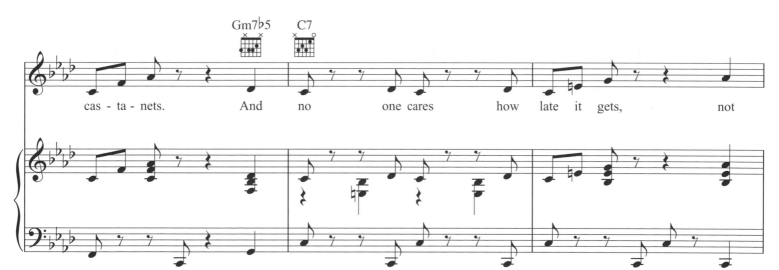

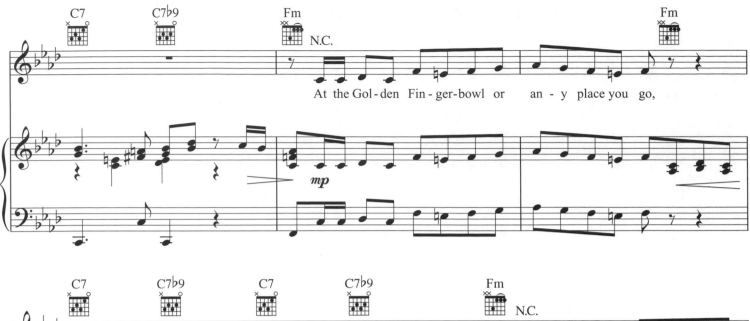

At the Gol-den Fin-ger-bowl or an-y place you go,

you will meet your Un-cle Max and

ev-'ry-one you know.

But if you go to the spot that I am think-in' of, you will be free

I'LL NEVER BE JEALOUS AGAIN

Words and Music by RICHARD ADLER
and JERRY ROSS

Tempo di Schottische (♩ = 112)

MABEL:

Pic - ture this. You're
Pic - ture this. You've

sit - ting and wait - ing for her to come back from a date. _____
noth - ing to do so you drop in to chat for a - while. _____

HINES:

There I am. I'm
There I am with

Here she comes. Her
Some - thing's up. The

sit - ting and wait - ing for her to come back from a date. _____
noth - ing to do so I drop in to chat for a - while. _____

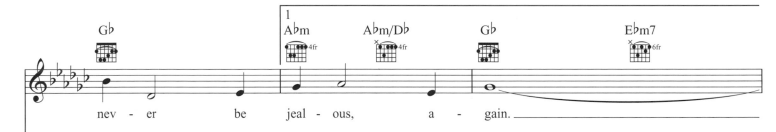

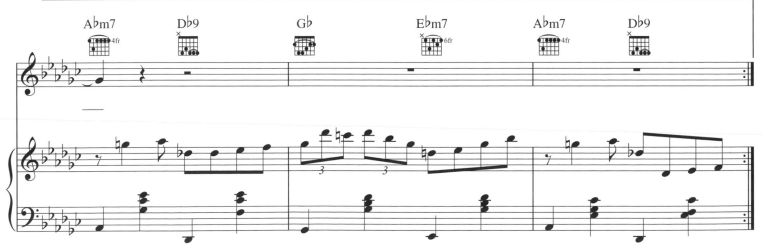

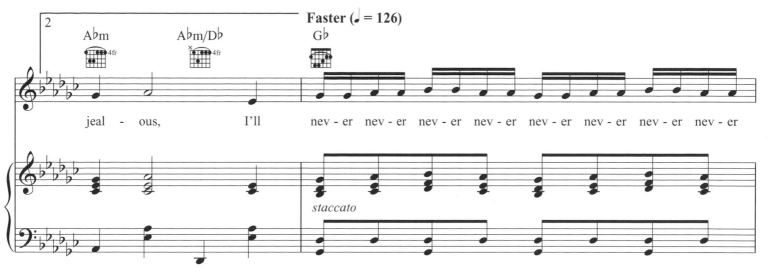

jeal - ous, I'll nev - er nev - er nev - er nev - er nev - er nev - er nev - er nev - er

nev - er be jeal - ous a - gain! There will be

no more night - mares to sleep through. No more

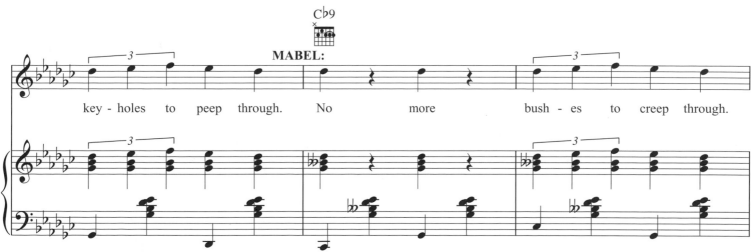

key - holes to peep through. No more bush - es to creep through.

Tempo I (♩ = 112)

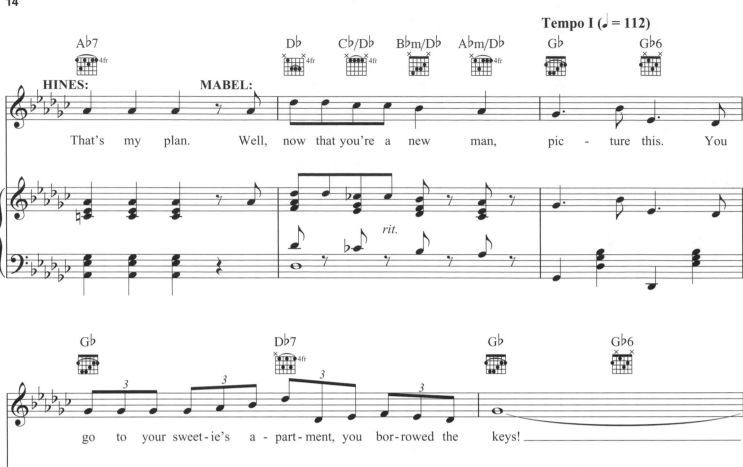

HINES: That's my plan. MABEL: Well, now that you're a new man, pic-ture this. You

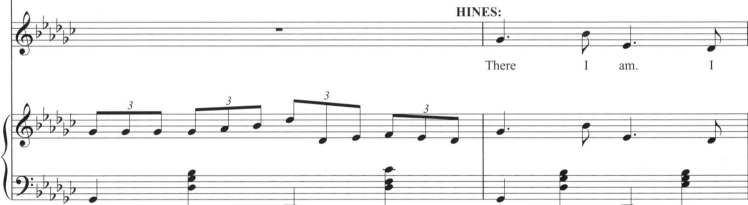

go to your sweet-ie's a-part-ment, you bor-rowed the keys!

HINES: There I am. I

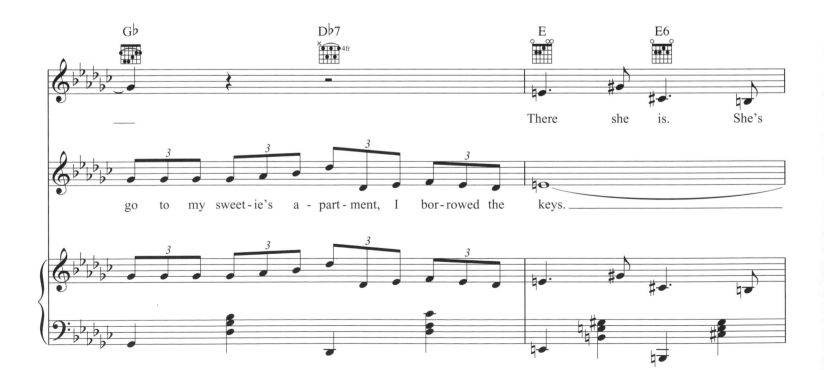

go to my sweet-ie's a-part-ment, I bor-rowed the keys.

There she is. She's

giv-ing a sail-or a ver-y af-fec-tion-ate squeeze.

There she is. She's

Then, to boot, she

giv-ing a sail-or a ver-y af-fec-tion-ate squeeze.

tells you she was in the arms of her cous-in who's back from o-ver-

I'M NOT AT ALL IN LOVE

Words and Music by RICHARD ADLER
and JERRY ROSS

Bright, in 1

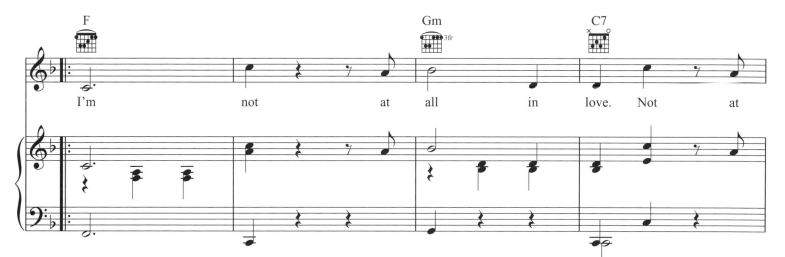

I'm not at all in love. Not at

all in love, not I. _____ Not a

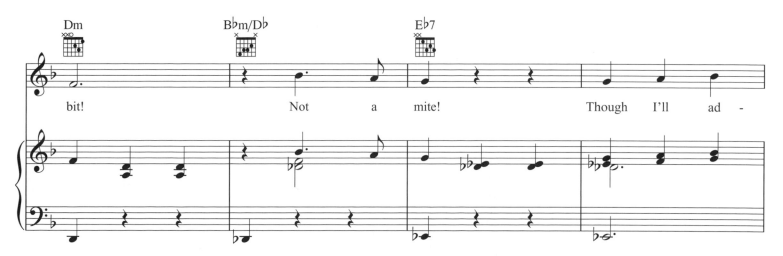

bit! Not a mite! Though I'll ad-

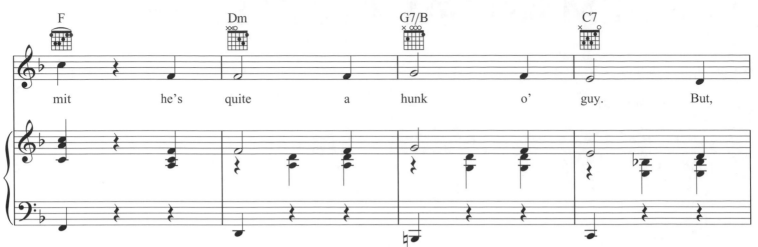

mit he's quite a hunk o' guy. But,

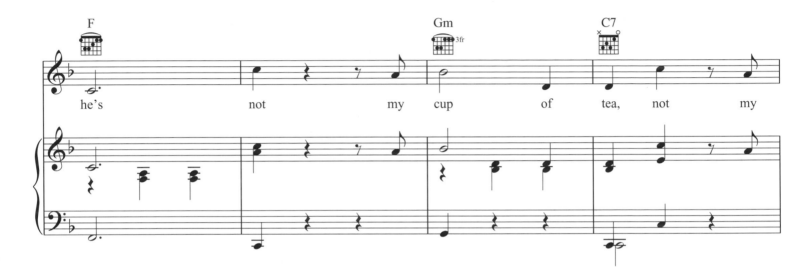

he's not my cup of tea, not my

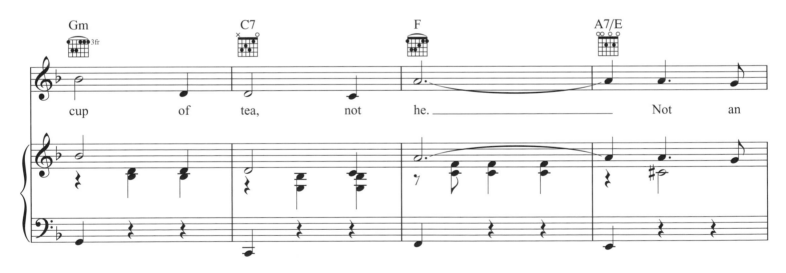

cup of tea, not he. _____ Not an

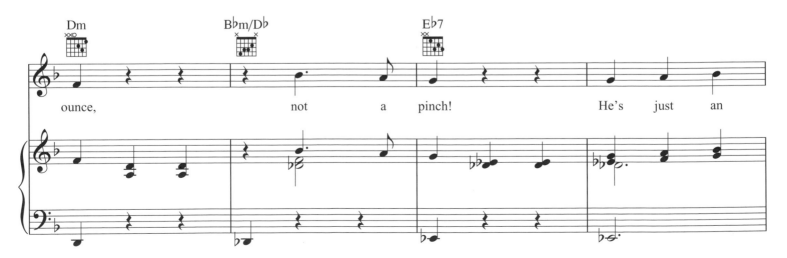

ounce, not a pinch! He's just an

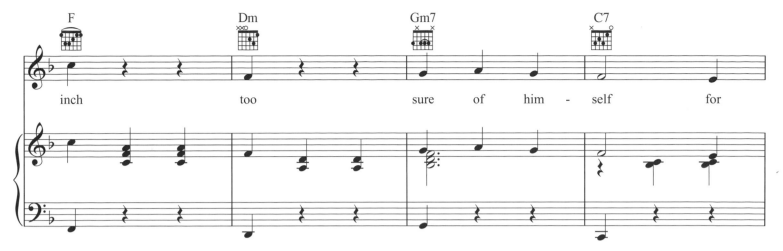

inch too sure of him-self for

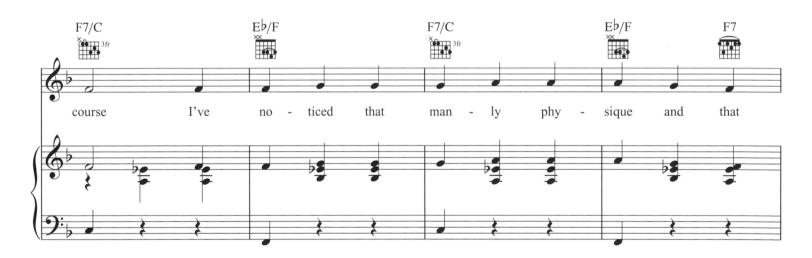

me! _____ Well of

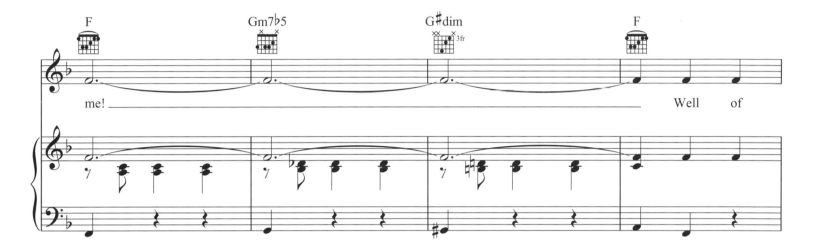

course I've no-ticed that man-ly phy-sique and that

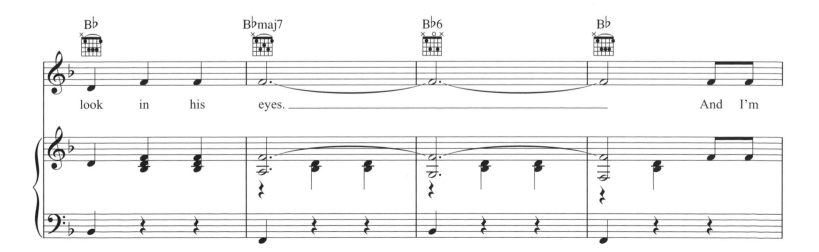

look in his eyes. _____ And I'm

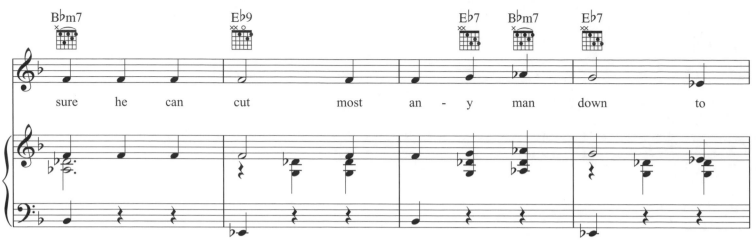

sure he can cut most an - y man down to

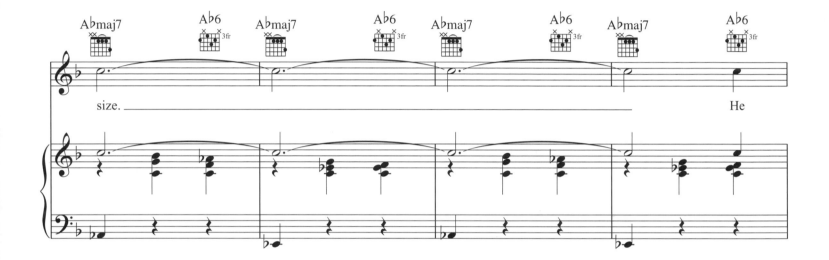

size. _____ He

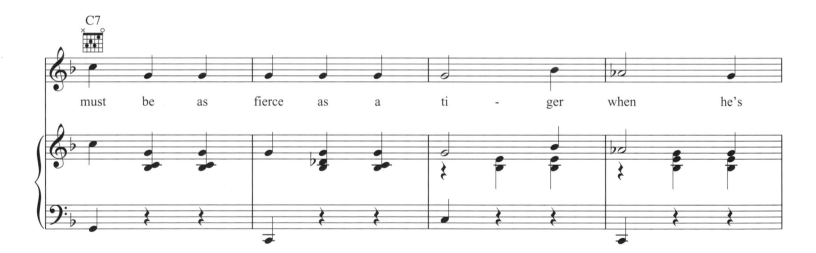

must be as fierce as a ti - ger when he's

mad. _____ And I'll

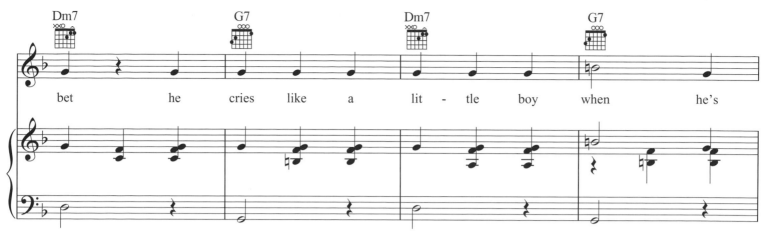

bet he cries like a lit - tle boy when he's

sad. _____ But

I'm not at all in love. Not at

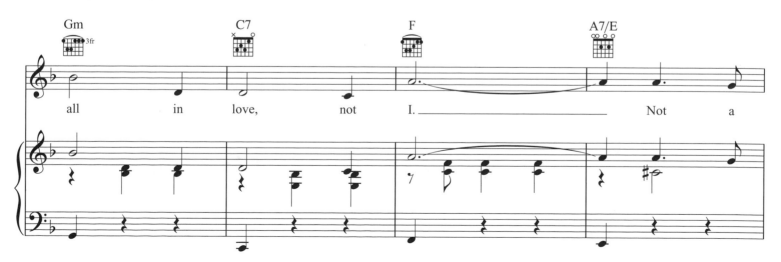

all in love, not I. _____ Not a

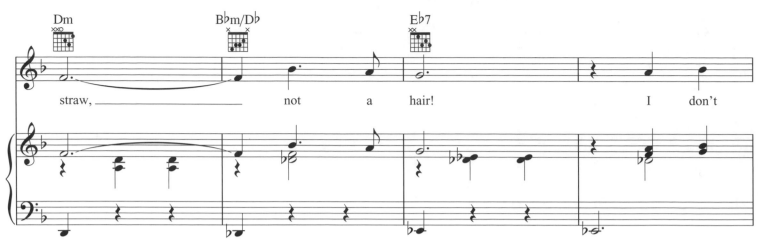

straw, _____ not a hair! I don't

care if he's as strong as a li - on,

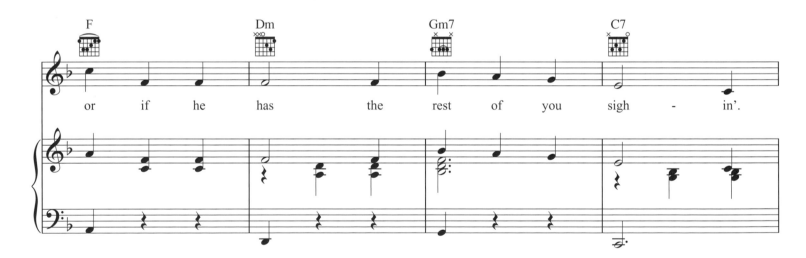

or if he has the rest of you sigh - in'.

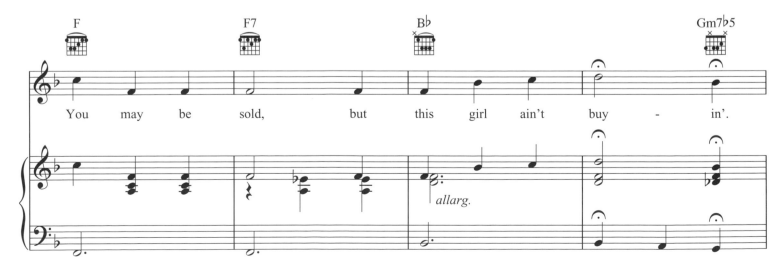

You may be sold, but this girl ain't buy - in'.

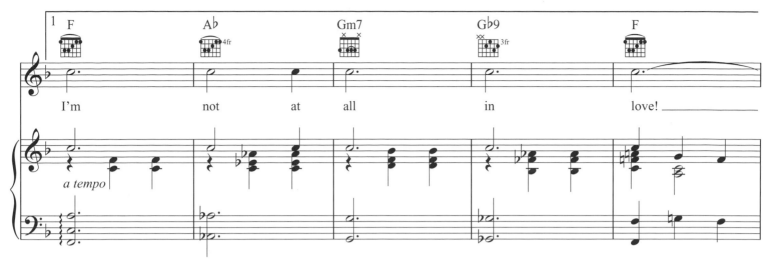

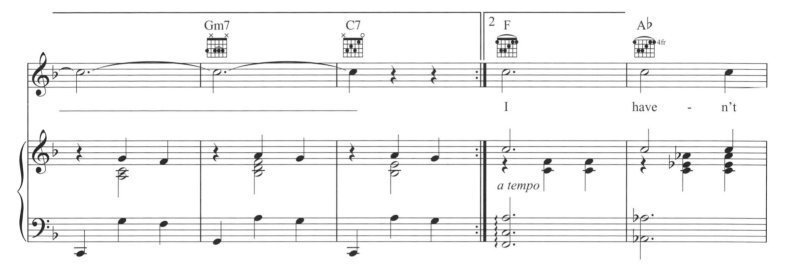

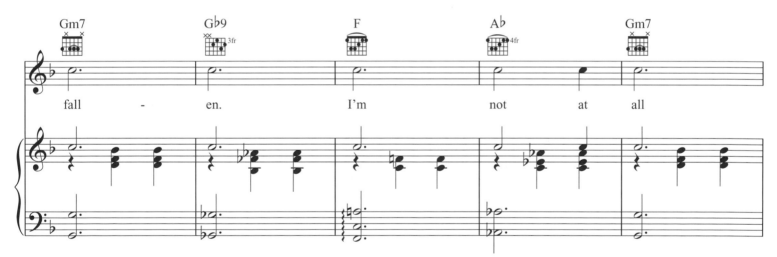

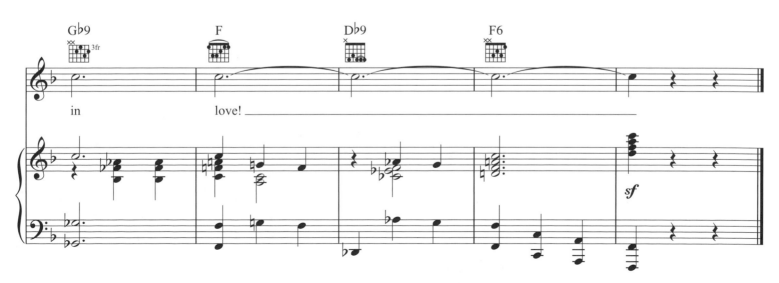

ONCE-A-YEAR-DAY

Words and Music by RICHARD ADLER
and JERRY ROSS

this   was   my   once - a - year day,   once - a -
This   is   my   once - a - year day,   once - a -

year day.   E - ven got a kiss from you. I feel like hop - pin' up and down,
year day.   Once a year we lose our sens - es. Look at Char - lie up a tree,

like a kan - ga - roo.   Jump - in' fenc - es, climb - in' trees. What please - es me is
kiss - in' Kat - ie's ear.   Char - lie's wife is mad as hell, oh well, it hap - pens

what I'll do, 'cause this   is   my ⎱   once - a - year day,
once - a - year. And this   is   that ⎰

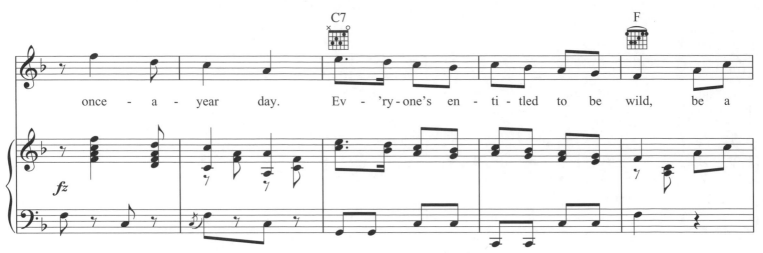

once - a - year day. Ev - 'ry-one's en - ti -tled to be wild, be a

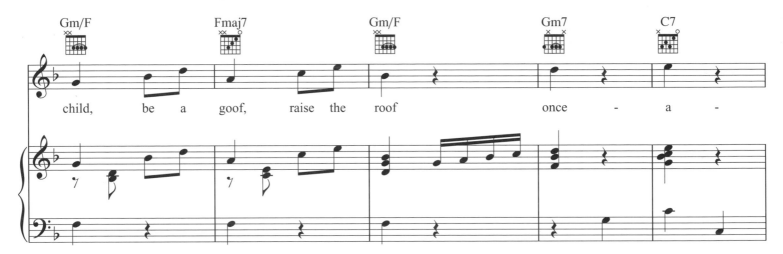

child, be a goof, raise the roof once - a -

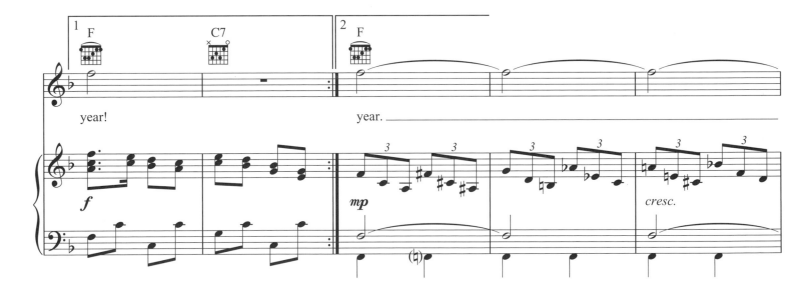

year! year. _____

STEAM HEAT

Words and Music by RICHARD ADLER
and JERRY ROSS

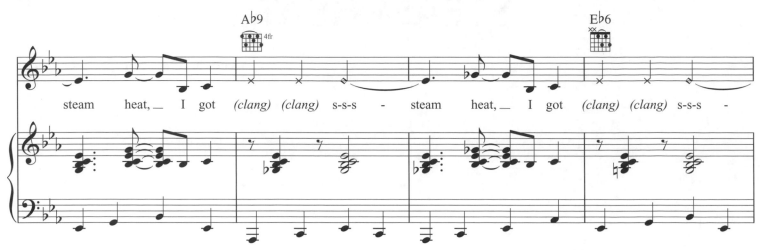

steam heat, __ I got (clang) (clang) s-s-s - steam heat, __ I got (clang) (clang) s-s-s -

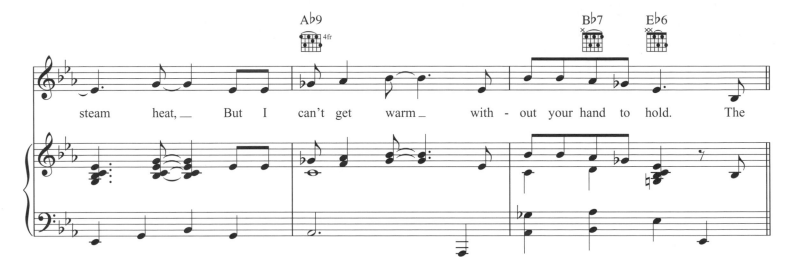

steam heat, __ But I can't get warm __ with - out your hand to hold. The

ra - di - a - tor's hiss - in', still I need your kiss - in' to keep me from freez - in' each

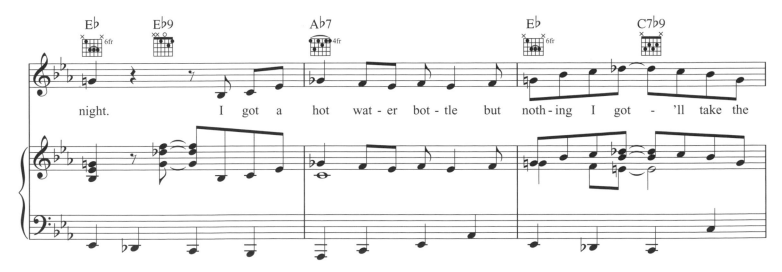

night. I got a hot wat - er bot - tle but noth - ing I got - 'll take the

place of you, ___ hold-ing me tight. I got *(clang)* *(clang)* s-s-s -

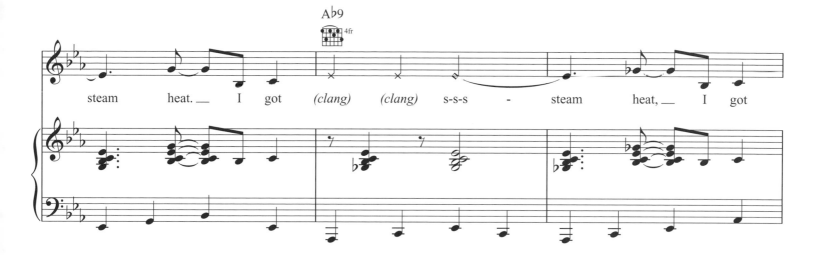

steam heat. ___ I got *(clang)* *(clang)* s-s-s - steam heat, ___ I got

(clang) *(clang)* s-s-s - steam heat. ___ But, I need your love ___ to

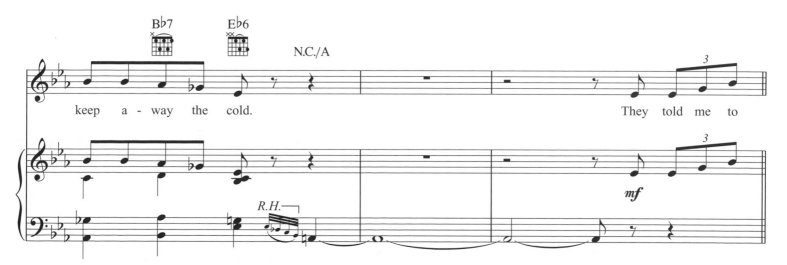

keep a - way the cold. They told me to

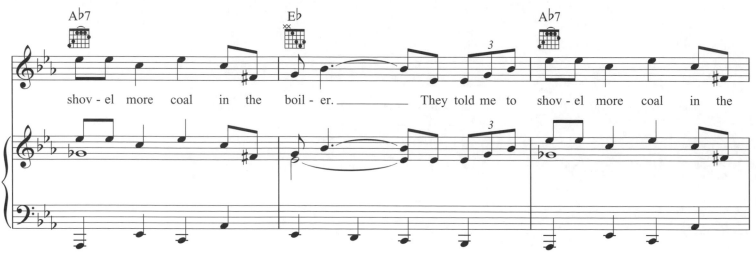

shov - el more coal in the boil - er._____ They told me to shov - el more coal in the

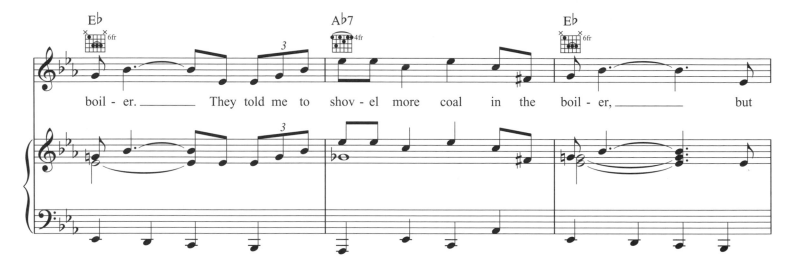

boil - er._____ They told me to shov - el more coal in the boil - er,_____ but

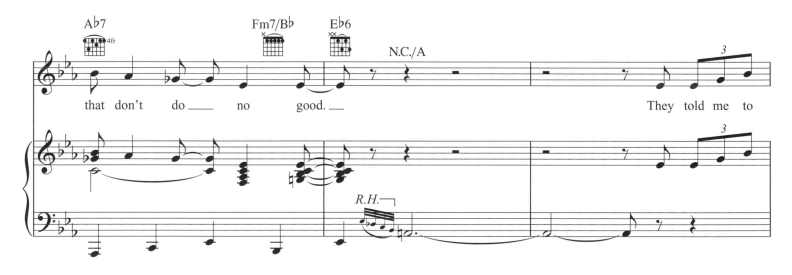

that don't do__ no good.__ They told me to

pour some more oil in the burn - er._____ They told me to pour some more oil in the

SEVEN-AND-A-HALF CENTS

Words and Music by RICHARD ADLER
and JERRY ROSS

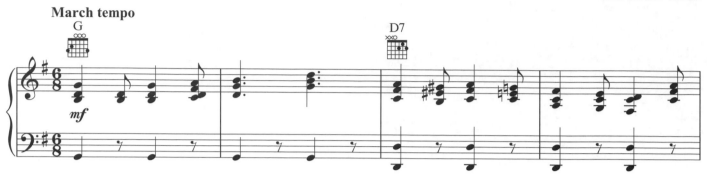

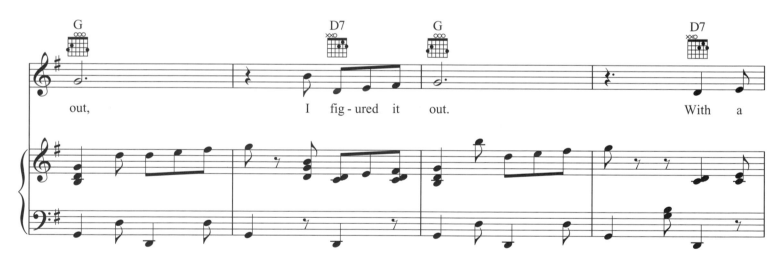

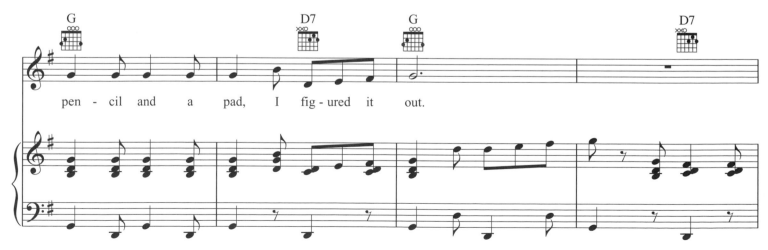

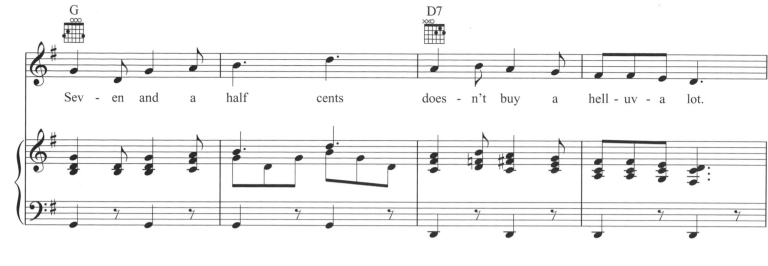

Sev - en and a half cents does - n't buy a hell - uv - a lot.

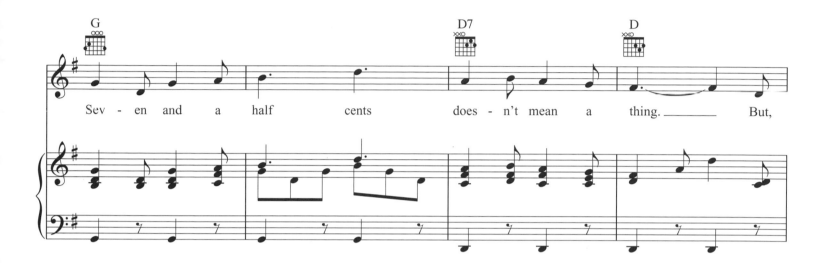

Sev - en and a half cents does - n't mean a thing. _____ But,

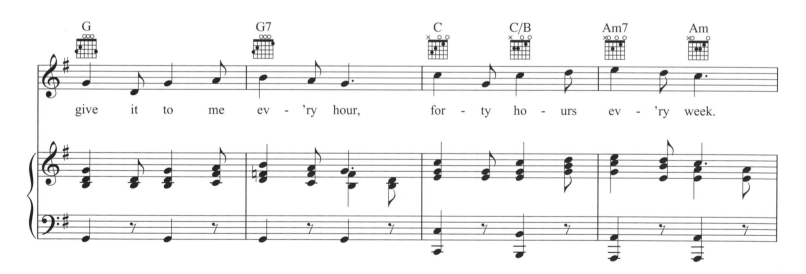

give it to me ev - 'ry hour, for - ty ho - urs ev - 'ry week.

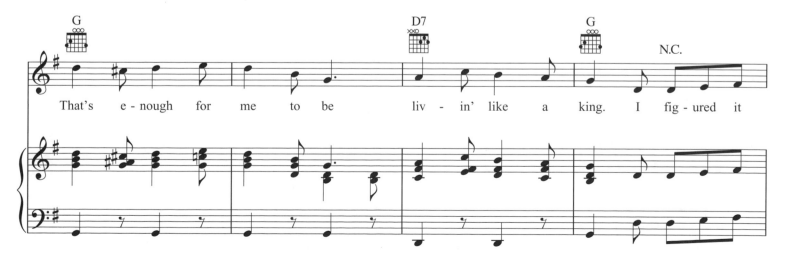

That's e - nough for me to be liv - in' like a king. I fig - ured it

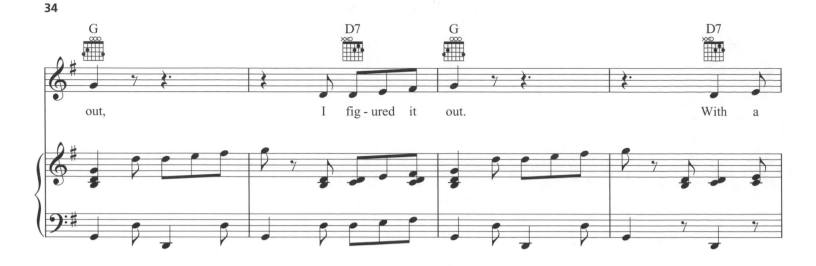

out,   I fig-ured it out.   With a

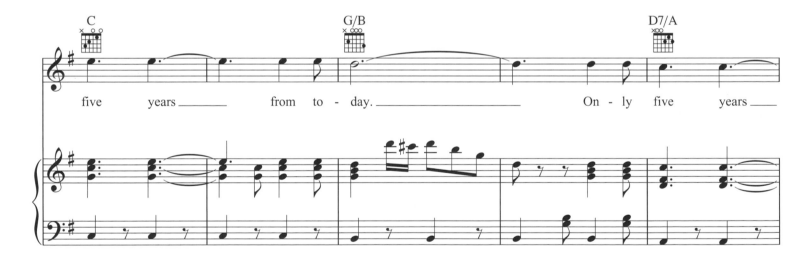

pen - cil and a pad, I fig-ured it out.   On - ly

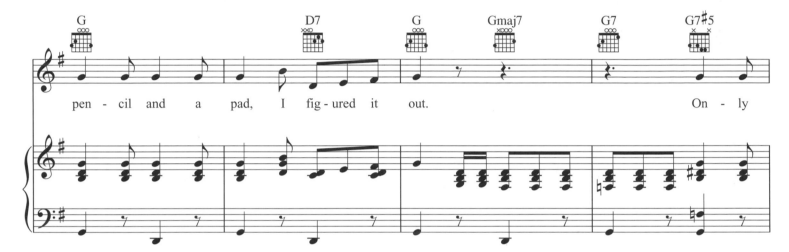

five   years _____ from to - day. _____ On - ly five   years _____

_____ from to - day. _____ I can see it _____ all be-

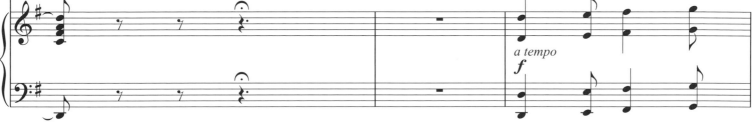

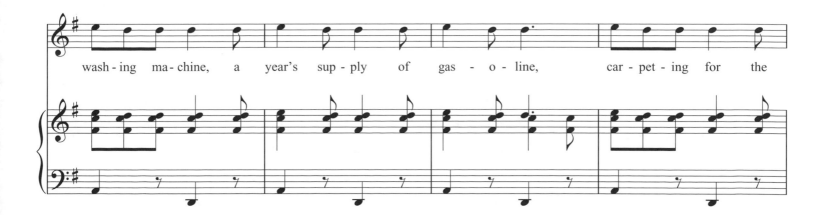

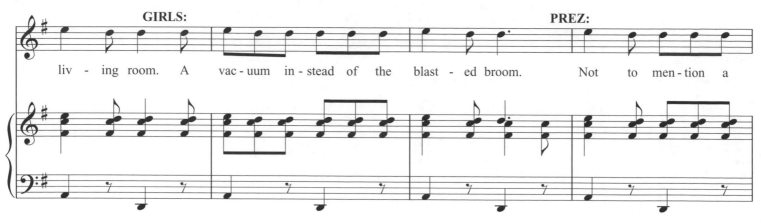

GIRLS: liv - ing room. A vac - uum in - stead of the blast - ed broom. **PREZ:** Not to men - tion a

for - ty inch tel - e - vi - sion set. **ALL:** So, al -

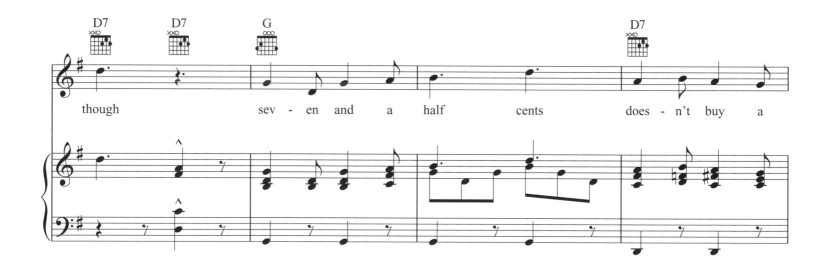

though sev - en and a half cents does - n't buy a

hell - uv - a lot, sev - en and a half cents does - n't mean a

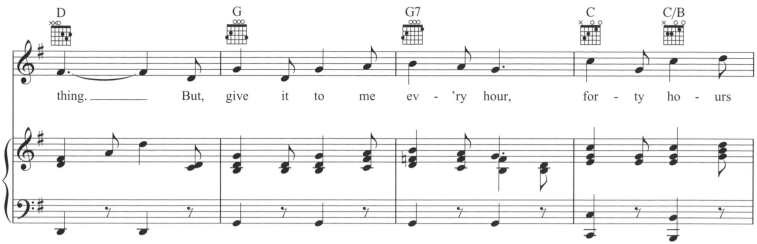

thing. _____ But, give it to me ev - 'ry hour, for - ty ho - urs

ev - 'ry week. That's e - nough for me to be liv - in' like a

BABE: king. I fig - ured it out. **ALL:** She fig - ured it out, she fig - ured it out. **BABE:** I fig - ured it

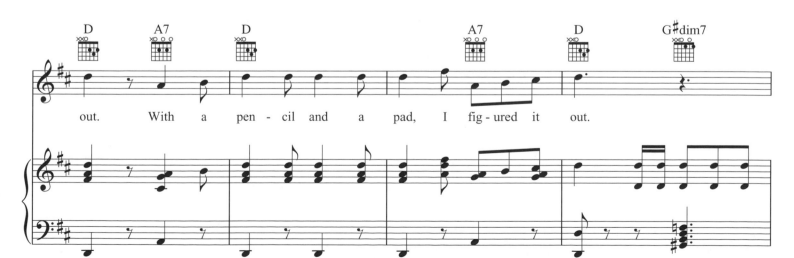

out. With a pen - cil and a pad, I fig - ured it out.

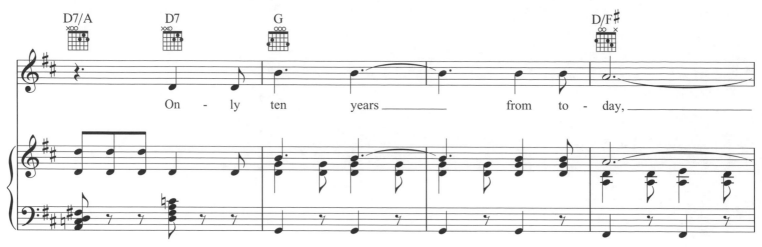

On - ly ten years _____ from to - day, _____

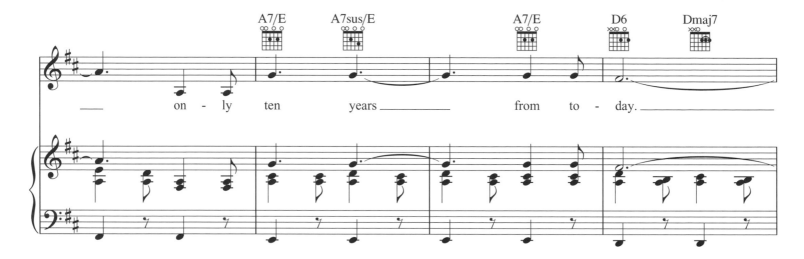

_____ on - ly ten years _____ from to - day. _____

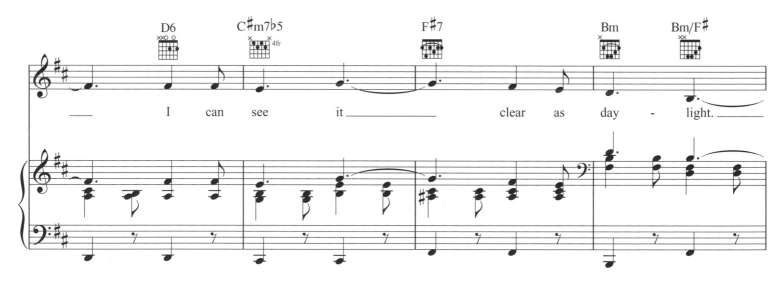

_____ I can see it _____ clear as day - light. _____

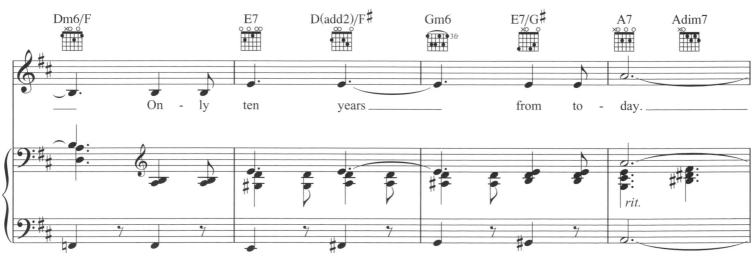

_____ On - ly ten years _____ from to - day. _____

rit.

A7   N.C.   ALL:

Spoken: Ten years... that's 520 weeks... times 40 hours every week... at roughly 2 1/4 hours overtime... at time and a half for overtime... comes to exactly... $1705.48.

Hoo-ray!

a tempo
f

BABE: A7

That's e-nough for me to buy a trip to France a-

p

cross the seas, a mo-tor-boat with wa-ter skis, may-be e-ven a

MEN: BABE:

for-eign car. A charge ac-count at the cor-ner bar. Not to men-tion a

Scrab - ble board with let - ters made of gold.   So,   al -

though   sev - en and   a   half   cents   does - n't   buy   a

ENSEMBLE:
We   fig - ured   it   out,   we   fig - ured   it   out.

hell - uv - a   lot,   sev - en and   a   half   cents   does - n't   mean   a

We   fig - ured   it   out,   we   fig - ured   it   out.

thing. _____ But, give it to me ev - 'ry hour, for - ty ho - urs

I fig - ure that give it to me ev - 'ry hour, for - ty ho - urs

ev - 'ry week. That's e - nough for me to be liv - in' like a

ev - 'ry week. That's e - nough for me to be liv - in' like a

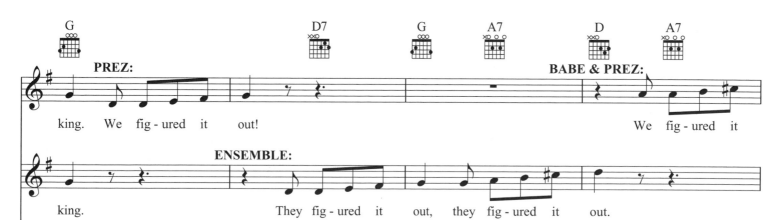

PREZ:

BABE & PREZ:

king. We fig - ured it out!

We fig - ured it

ENSEMBLE:

king. They fig - ured it out, they fig - ured it out.

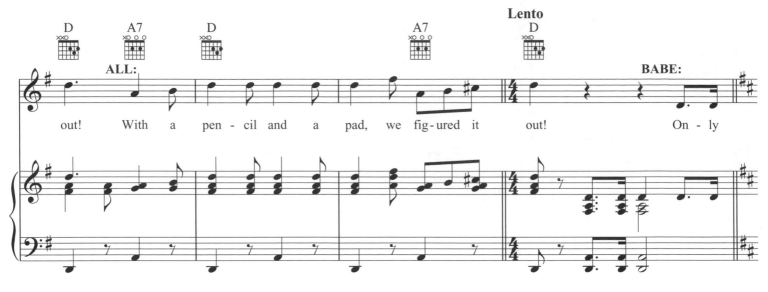

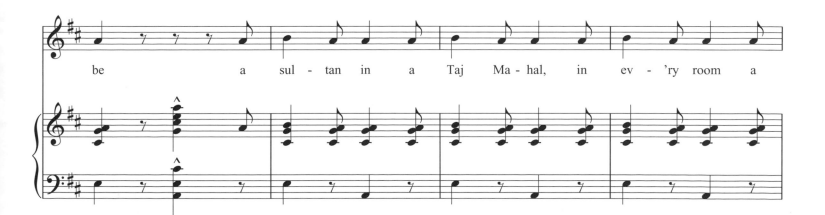

BABE:

dif - f'rent doll. I'll have my - self a buy - in' spree, I'll buy a pa - ja - ma

fac - to - ry. Then I could end up hav - in' old man Has - ler work for

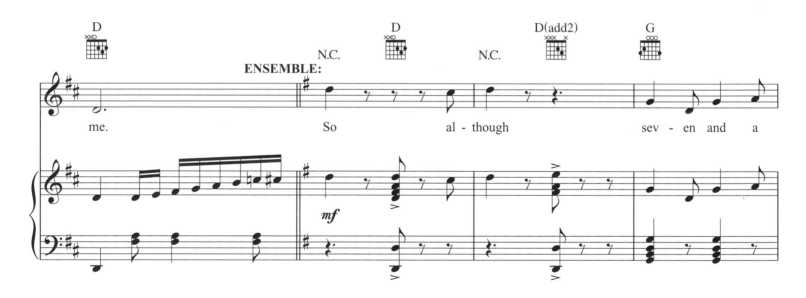

ENSEMBLE:

me. So al - though sev - en and a

half cents does - n't buy a hell - uv - a lot, sev - en and a

half cents does - n't mean a thing. _____ But, give it to me

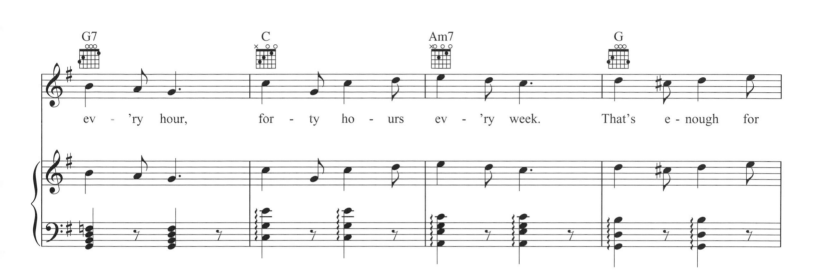

ev - 'ry hour, for - ty ho - urs ev - 'ry week. That's e - nough for

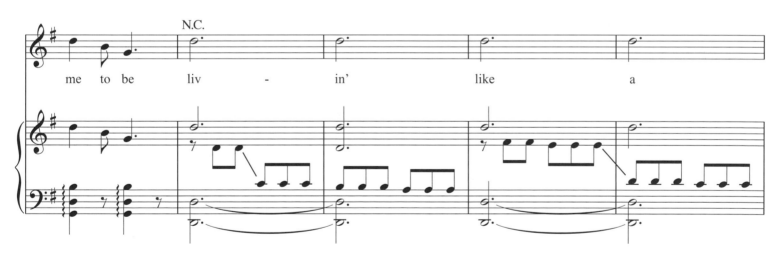

me to be liv - in' like a

king! _____

SMALL TALK

Words and Music by RICHARD ADLER
and JERRY ROSS

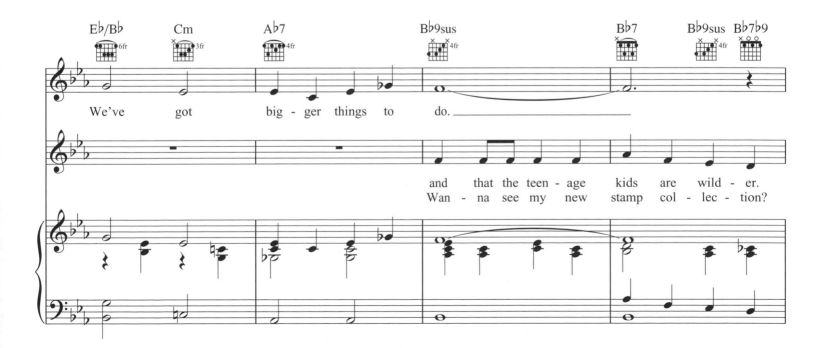

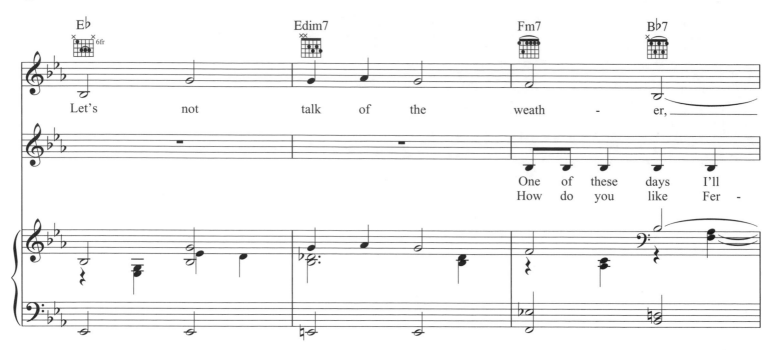

Let's not talk of the weath - er,

One of these days I'll
How do you like Fer -

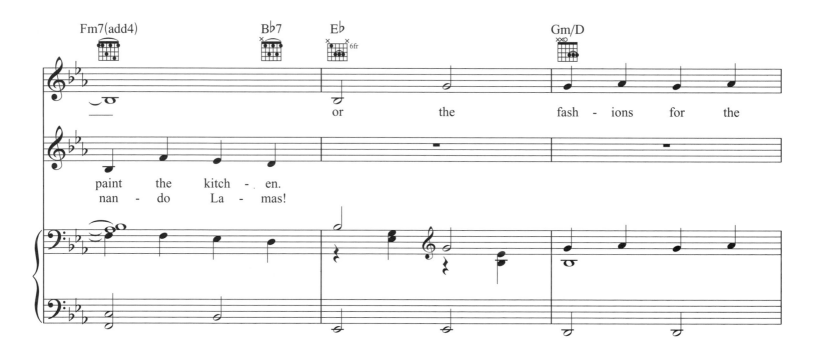

or the fash - ions for the

paint the kitch - en.
nan - do La - mas!

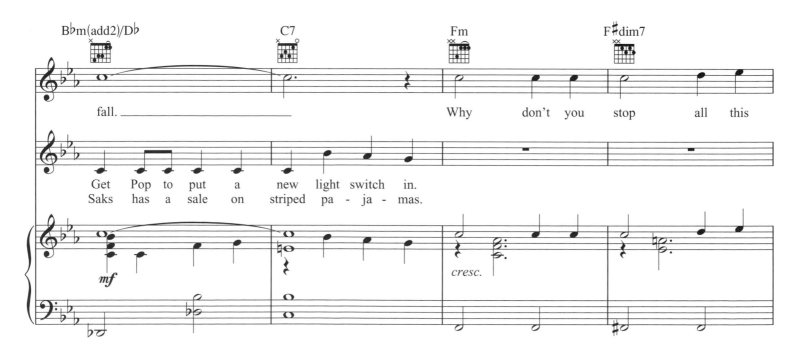

fall. _____

Why don't you stop all this

Get Pop to put a new light switch in.
Saks has a sale on striped pa - ja - mas.

small talk? I've got some-thing bet - ter for

Like I was say - in'... What I mean is...
Like I was say - in'... What I mean is...

your lips to do, and that takes no talk at

I was on - ly... Well...
I was on - ly... Well...

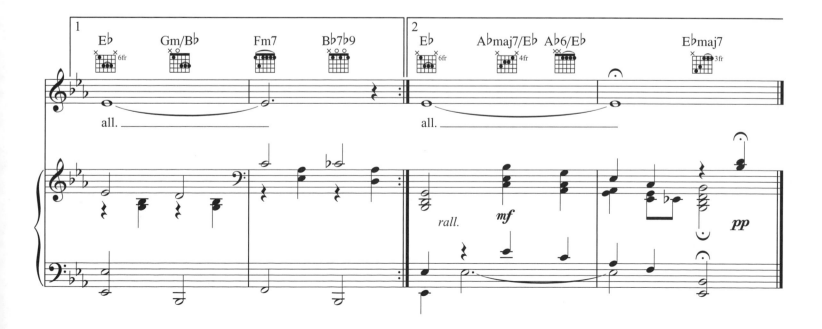

all. _____

all. _____

THERE ONCE WAS A MAN

Words and Music by RICHARD ADLER
and JERRY ROSS

Bright tempo

(Man:) There

once was a man _____ who loved a
once was a wom-an _____ who loved a

wom- an. _____
man. _____

She was the one he slew a drag - on for! ____
He was the one that she took poi - son for! ____

They say that no - bod - y ev - er loved as much as
They say that no - bod - y ev - er loved as much as

he - ee, ____ but
she - ee, ____ but

me - ee. ____ I love you
me - ee. ____ I love you

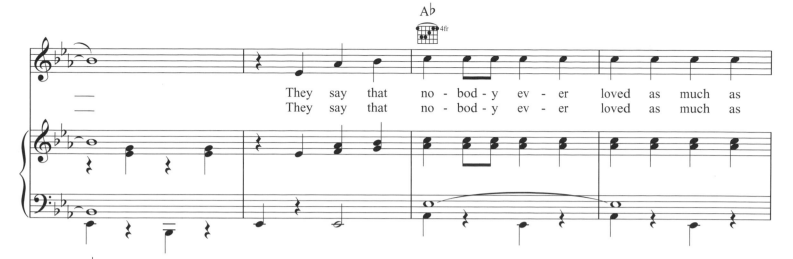

They say that no-bod-y ev-er loved as much as
They say that no-bod-y ev-er loved as much as

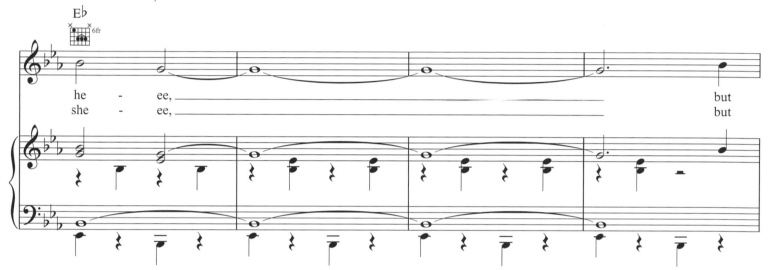

he - ee, ___ but
she - ee, ___ but

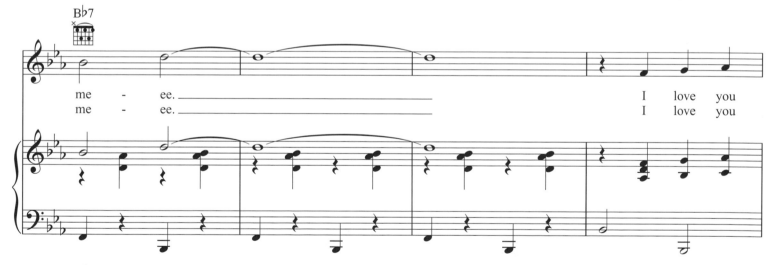

me - ee. ___ I love you
me - ee. ___ I love you

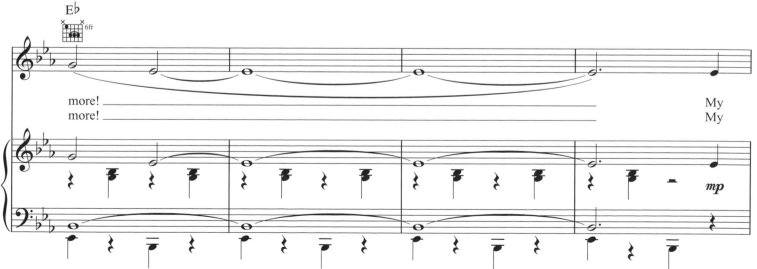

more! ___ My
more! ___ My

love is a gi - ant, fierce and de - fi - ant. But,
love's me - te - or - ic. It's mere - ly his - tor - ic, a

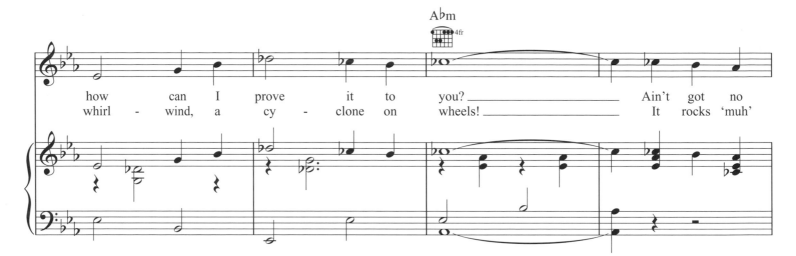

how can I prove it to you?_____ Ain't got no
whirl - wind, a cy - clone on wheels!_____ It rocks 'muh'

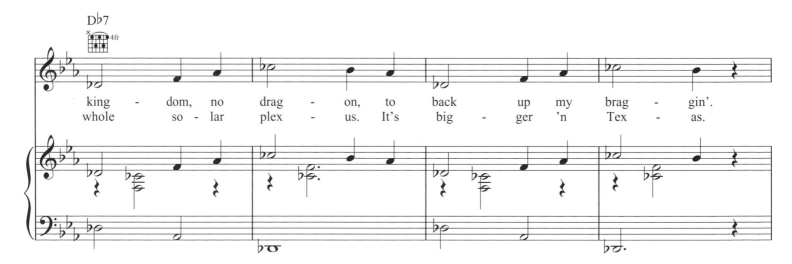

king - dom, no drag - on, to back up my brag - gin'.
whole so - lar plex - us. It's big - ger 'n Tex - as.

How can I show what I would do? I on - ly know there
I just can't tell you how it feels! I on - ly know there